MW01672105

Sex Positions

Discover Kama Sutra Techniques and Sex Toys to Improve your Relationship

Florinda Besancon

Table of Contents

© Copyright 2021 by Florinda Besancon- All rights reserved.

The following Book is reproduced below with the goal of providing information that is as accurate and reliable as possible. Regardless, purchasing this Book can be seen as consent to the fact that both the publisher and the author of this book are in no way experts on the topics discussed within and that any recommendations or suggestions that are made herein are for entertainment purposes only. Professionals should be consulted as needed prior to undertaking any of the action endorsed herein.

This declaration is deemed fair and valid by both the American Bar Association and the Committee of Publishers Association and is legally binding throughout the United States.

Furthermore, the transmission, duplication, or reproduction of any of the following work including specific information will be considered an illegal act irrespective of if it is done electronically or in print. This extends to creating a secondary or tertiary copy of the work or a recorded copy and is only allowed with the express written consent from the Publisher. All additional right reserved.

The information in the following pages is broadly considered a truthful and accurate account of facts and as such, any inattention, use, or misuse of the information in question by the reader will render any resulting actions solely under their purview. There are no scenarios in which the publisher or the original author of this work can be in any fashion deemed liable for any hardship or damages that may befall them after undertaking information described herein.

Additionally, the information in the following pages is intended only for informational purposes and should thus be thought of as universal. As befitting its nature, it is presented without assurance regarding its prolonged validity or interim quality. Trademarks that are mentioned are done without written consent and can in no way be considered an endorsement from the trademark holder.

Introduction

It is unlikely that you have never heard of the Kama sutra before, but you may be unfamiliar with what exactly it is. Some may think of it as simply a book of sex positions, while others may know a bit more of the history and how it came to be.

This part will look at the history behind the Kama Sutra, discussing the literal meaning of the words, as well as what it teaches us, and how it is meant to be used. Since the Kama Sutra originated in India, there are also many terms and words used throughout that you may not be familiar with, so we will make sure to breakdown some of the most commonly seen ones and provide their definitions.

When it comes to sex, communication is key there, as well. This is especially true when in a long-term relationship. When having casual sex, communication is helpful; since then, you can figure out what the person likes and dislikes, but oftentimes it takes trial and error to find out how to please that person. Likely, by the time you figure out exactly how to do so, you have moved onto the next person. When having sex in a relationship, you have much more time to talk about sex and find out what that person likes and dislikes.

At one time or another, you likely had a fiery sex life with your partner, but over time it slowly dwindles as relationships settle in and people become comfortable with one another. Alternatively, you may be fresh in a relationship and keep seeking advice on how to have a strong sex life from the get-go. Regardless of where you are, in life, and experience, this book can help you experience great joy in your sex life.

If you are ready to level up your experience and add fiery passion and romance to your relationship, then you have come to the right place. This book will provide you with excellent advice for both inside and outside of the bedroom, as well as some awesome new sex positions for you to try. Altogether, you will have everything you need to spark fierce and romantic passion in your relationship once again.

CHAPTER 1:

Sex Toys for Couples

Sex toys and tools are a fun addition to enhance your sex life. The following are a variety of toys and tools that can be used by couples to spice up the bedroom life. These toys can be used simply for fun or as a part of role-playing. Sex toys tend to increase the amount of stimulation being experienced by one or both partners, creating more explosive orgasms. They can also enhance the intimacy between lovers, as you learn what each other enjoy most.

Vibrating Panties

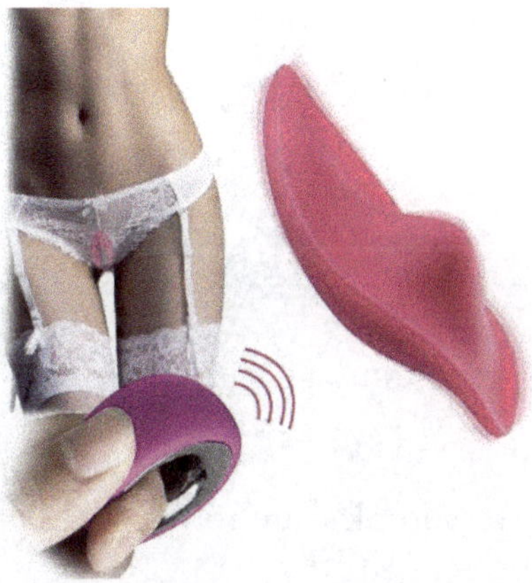

These are a fun way to encourage foreplay long before you even hit the bedroom. Vibrating panties that have a remote-control feature can be worn on a date night, with the gentleman controlling the remote control. He can then turn it on and off at his own desire, having his lady at his mercy until he is ready to have his way with her. These can also be awesome if you purchase a crotchless panty variety, as they can stay on and turned-on during sex to continue the stimulation throughout the encounter.

Vibrating Wand

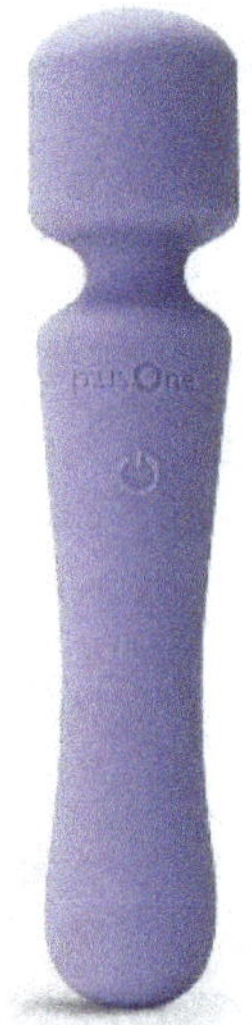

Wands are a fun way to add pleasure to the sexual experience. You can apply as much or as little pressure as you desire, and either partner can be in control of the wand. It can be used on either partner and doesn't have to be limited to the sex organs. To enhance the experience, you can trace your partner's inner thighs or butt with the wand while it is switched on.

Cock Ring

There is a variety of different cock rings available on the market. They are believed to assist gentlemen in lasting longer and help make them rock hard. If you are just looking for a simple cock ring, there is a variety of silicone types that are stretchy and apply or remove easily. Alternatively, you can purchase a vibrating cock ring that can provide stimulation to her clitoris with each thrust while also providing a consistent vibrate to his penis during sex.

Butt Plugs or Anal Beads

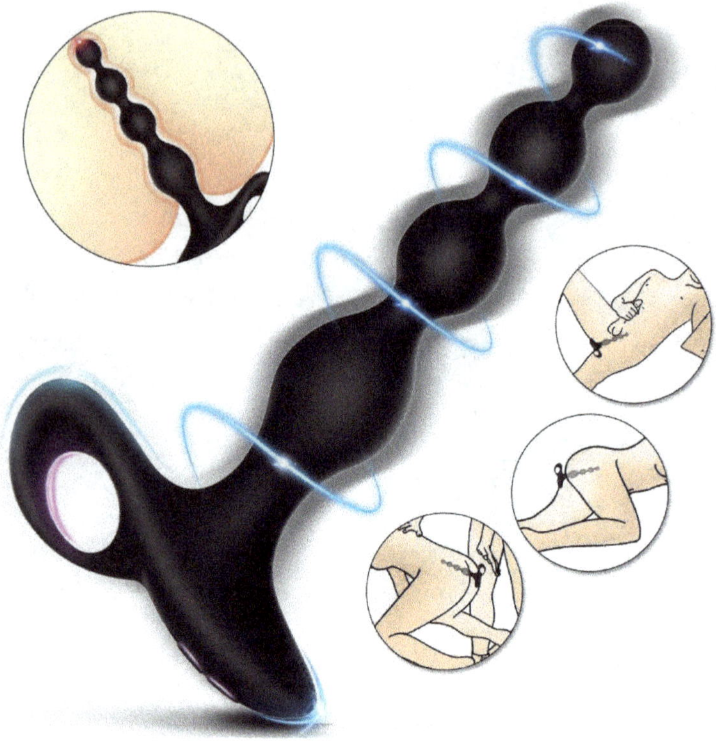

If you are into anal play, butt plugs and anal beads come in a variety of fun forms. There are butt plugs with rhinestones on them, butt plugs shaped like hooks, small ones, large ones; there are anal beads that increasingly get larger or several same-sized ones on a string. There are several anal-play toys that can be used during vaginal penetration to create a double penetration experience for the woman. This can also be enjoyable for the man, as he can typically feel it against his penis while he penetrates her vagina and can even make it feel tighter and more textured for him.

Floggers

There are a variety of floggers and whips that can create an enjoyable bedroom experience for those interested in a BDSM-style adventure. It is important that if you use these toys, you realize that they are not intended to be used with great force, but rather with gentle but consistent force. You do not want to cause bodily harm to your lover. That being said, a good spanking with a flogger can add many levels of pleasure to your sex.

Feather Tickler

These, as well as other textured toys, are excellent for stimulating the senses while having sex. They can be used in virtually any way to entice senses that aren't normally triggered during sex. For example, you can blindfold your partner and then trace their body with the feather tickler, or you can gently run it over their penis or vagina to increase blood flow to their sex organs and turn them on even more. The opportunities are endless with these types of toys.

Bondage Straps

These straps come in a variety of different shapes and sizes and are used to help support the submissive during bondage sex moves. Some of these straps include ones to help support the tummy to keep their bum up high, some that keep legs high, or ones that keep arms behind their back. You can find these on any number of sex toy sites that sell bondage gear.

Lingerie

Believe it or not, sexy ensembles are not strictly for women to wear. Although there is a vast number of lingerie outfits for women to wear for her man, there are also many for men to wear. Adding lingerie is an incredible way to enhance sexual pleasure. You can even use lingerie to dress up in certain roles and include role-playing in your intimate encounters. Some inspiration for role-playing includes doctor and patient, cop and prisoner, secretary and boss, or anything else that turns you on and helps liven up your sexy time.

Blind Folds

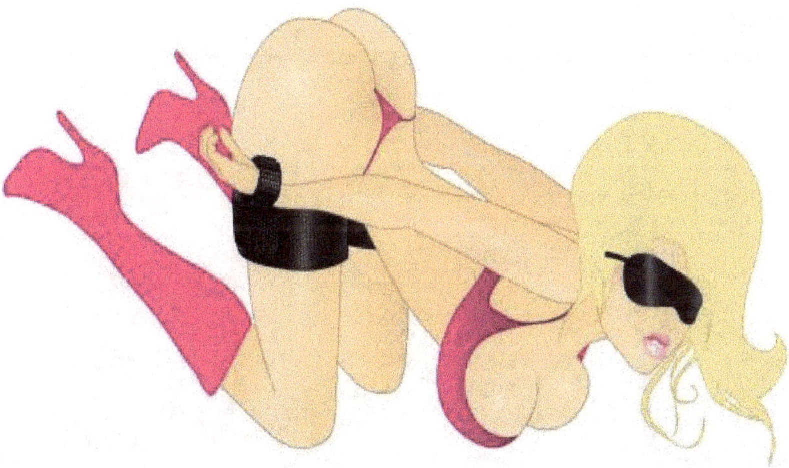

There is a certain level of mystery that comes with using blindfolds during sex. The blindfolded partner will experience increased physical awareness as they are no longer able to see what is happening to them. It enhances the excitement with every touch they experience while also removing the element of expecting what is yet to come. When your partner is blindfolded, you can add to their pleasure by using a variety of different textured items to stimulate sensitive areas on their body. (I.e., feather on the thighs, silk on the lower back, pearls on the chest, etc.)

Hand Cuffs or Rope

Having your partner tied down or restricted can greatly enhance their sexual pleasure. It takes away from their ability to react, almost forcing them to take anything you must give them. It can be an exciting way to take control in the bedroom and enjoy a BDSM experience. Almost everyone has some level of desire to be tied down and have someone else take their way with them. However, make sure your partner is on board with this as you should never do something your partner does not want to do.

Sex Swing

There are several swings made specifically for sex that can deeply enhance the sexual experience. You will need to have a solid place to mount your swing, but they can create a wonderful opportunity to create a more fluid movement for penetration. Also, they generally have customizable settings so you can control the height and the way in which the person sitting in the swing is positioned. They are a wonderful addition to any intimate bedroom!

Girth Enhancers

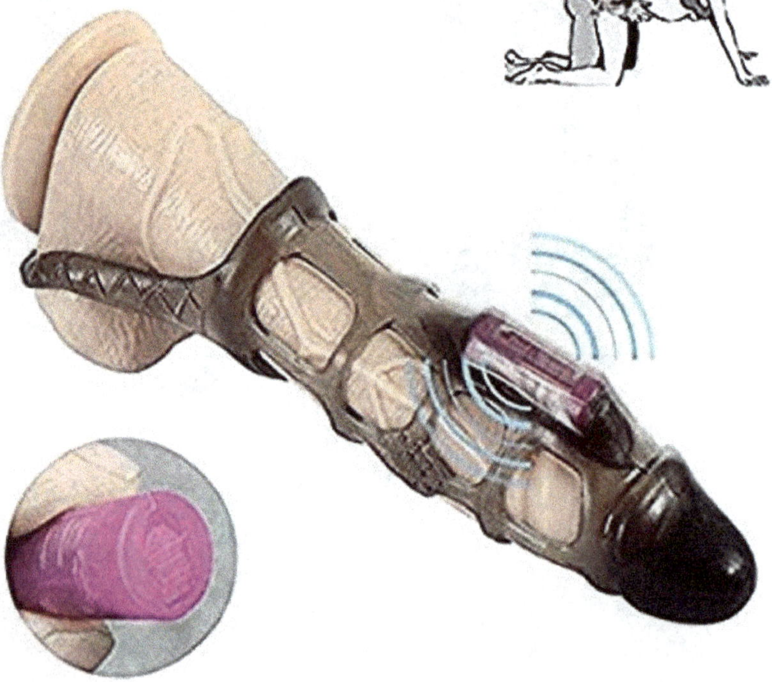

While these aren't for everyone, they are out there. These toys are similar to cock rings, except they're longer and thicker. They generally help the gentleman last much longer while also filling the woman up much more. They resemble dildos, except they have a hole in the center where the gentleman's penis fits inside. Girth enhancers can be a fun way to change up the pace and style and can even be a part of role-playing to make it feel as though you are with someone else entirely.

Nipple Clamps

These clamps are generally set only to squeeze a certain amount and are applied to the nipples during sex. They help to stimulate other areas of the body and increase the amount of pleasure felt by the wearer. While they are traditionally used by females, there are many males who enjoy wearing nipple clamps as well. Nipples are a very sensitive part of the body, so including them in sex can help have a full body orgasm.

"Hot Seats" or Sex Chairs

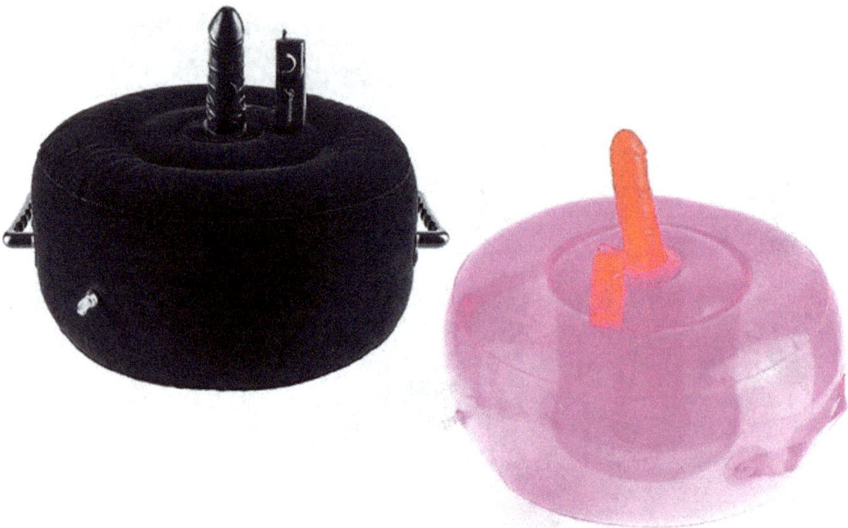

These chairs are generally little round poufs that have a dildo in the center. The dildo can be used to achieve a double-penetration experience for the female. They are generally blow-up chairs that have no sides or backings, so you can position yourself in whatever way is comfortable for you. They are easy to put up and take down and are wonderful for anyone looking for something different and with maximum pleasure for her if she's OK with anal.

Oral Sex Stimulators

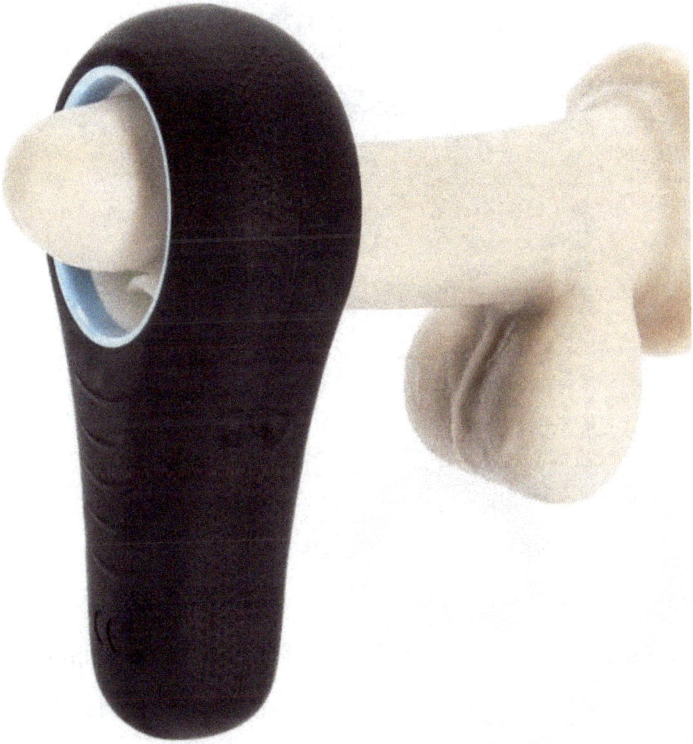

Similar to vibrating toys, these toys feature several little tongue-shaped pieces that spin quickly to create the sensation of receiving oral pleasure. They are wonderful for couples as they can be used to stimulate the lady's clitoris during sex to increase her chances of having an orgasm. They can also be used in other areas of the body to stimulate sensations that aren't normally felt during sex, to create a full-body experience further.

Paddles

Paddles can be made from a variety of materials, including leather, wood, metal, and more. They are generally smaller, hand-held toys that look exactly how they sound: like paddles. These are used to spank your partner and can be used anywhere on their body. The most common places include the cheeks, their bottom, and their feet. Always take care to use the tool gently, as you do not want to cause bruising or harm to your partner. This toy is not to abuse your partner but rather to stimulate a naughty sensation. You always want to use light but consistent pressure when you're using it. Make sure you're extra gentle if you're using it on their face and that they approve of such things before you try. You do not want your partner to be, feel, or look as though they are being abused!

Electric Stimulation Toys

These toys are a little bit pricier but work by sending subtle but noticeable electric shocks through your partner. When used properly, they are not dangerous and can greatly enhance the sensation of a full-body experience. They are perfect for stimulating parts of the body that are otherwise neglected during sex. You can purchase these from almost any sex store, and they can be used on either partner. They are a fun and unique addition to your sex life if this is the type of thing you are interested in.

CHAPTER 2:

Kama Sutra Erotic Massage

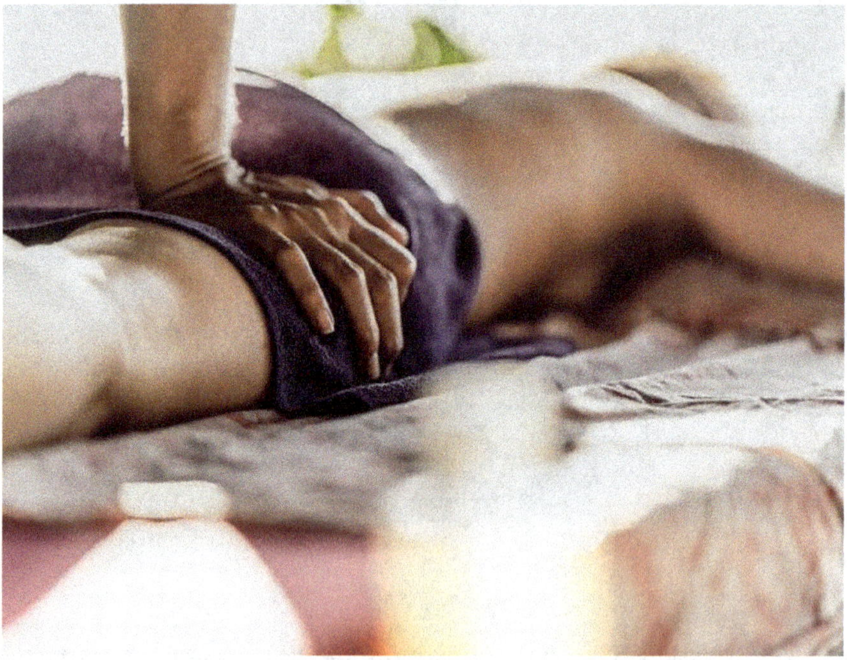

The Kama Sutra talks about massages and the best places to give massages. Some massages will lead to sex, and some will not. A massage can also be a relaxing gesture of love for your partner, who is spending time with you at the end of the day. If you have massage oil, this will be a great addition, but if not, that's okay too. Use something like lotion to lubricate your hands and avoid skin to skin friction. Warm your hands before you start so that it makes them feel nice and doesn't send a chill down their spine when you first make contact.

When they are lying in a comfortable position, and you have lubricated your hands, begin to massage them gently. The touch of a massage gives a person a sense of being cared for, and it is even better from the person they love. A massage is a great way to show your partner that you care about making them feel good. After you have massaged their upper body or their feet, begin kissing their body where you just massaged it and then progress to kissing them on the lips. You can gradually move into touching each other's genitals or massaging them there. This is when it becomes an erotic massage. You can give a woman or a man to lead them to immense pleasure and enjoy a very sensual experience with them. An erotic massage is a way to show love to a partner, a way to be sexually intimate together, and a way to make a person feel great without having a penis and vagina meet. Knowing these techniques is great for anyone who is looking to try new ways of pleasuring your partner in the bedroom.

Tips to Give an Erotic Massage to Him

A sort of erotic massage that you can try giving to a male partner is the prostate massage. As you know now, the prostate is a small gland located inside a man's body between the base of his penis and his anus. It is accessed through the anus. This type of massage is similar to anal play, but it is not the same, as the goals are different, and so is the technique.

The reason why it is better to give a man an erotic message here instead of on his penis is that he will be able to last much longer without reaching orgasm.

Performing this type of massage requires lots of lube for maximum comfortability. Once your fingers are well-lubricated, you can slide a finger or two inside of the man's anus very slowly. Once in, you will be able to find the prostate by feeling around on the upper (front) wall of the rectum for a small lump that is rough in texture a few inches deep. Once you have found it, you can begin to massage it gently. You can move your fingers in circles and apply light pressure to them. This massage has the potential to feel quite pleasurable for the man. Communicate while the massage is occurring in order to give him the most pleasure possible.

This massage does not need to lead to orgasm; at least, that is not the goal. If it happens, that is fine; however, the aim of this massage is just to provide a relaxing and pleasurable experience for him.

Tips to Give an Erotic Massage to Her

This massage involves the entire vaginal area, which is called the vulva. A Yoni Massage is a vaginal massage that is intended to open up the woman to her sexuality, her pleasure, and her sexual desires. As a partner, you can perform this type of massage for your woman to unlock her repressed sexual energy and help her to get in touch with it.

This can be done in a variety of ways, but the position we are going to discuss is a hot water Yoni Massage. Begin by setting the ambiance, either in the bathroom with a bathtub or around your jacuzzi. Set up some candles, some flowers, or anything that will make the surroundings relaxing and calm. Begin by having her breathe deeply and focus on her body and its sensations. You can get into the water with her for added intimacy. Begin by slowly and gently massaging around her entire vulva and her clitoral area. The key to this type of massage is to do everything very slowly. Begin to massage her clitoris slowly and not with the intention of making her come. When ready, and with lots of waterproof lube, slide one finger inside of her vagina and gently begin massaging the upper wall. Here is where her G-spot is located. Encourage her to express and release any sounds she naturally makes. Move your finger in a circular motion slowly and with your other hand, massage her pelvic area and clitoris. This connects the inner with the outer. Continue to do this and let the experience unfold with no end goal in mind. If she reaches orgasm, she can do so, but if she doesn't, she can just enjoy the pleasures that she is getting from your massage.

After this massage, she will feel more in touch with her body, and if penetrative sex ensues, both of you will feel even more pleasure and intensity of orgasms due to how engorged and activated her vagina and clitoris will be.

CHAPTER 3:

Seduction

What Seduction Is

Many times, our curiosity pushes us towards the word "seduction." Understanding its meaning, techniques, skills, examples of people who, in an innate way, are more likely to attract or seduce someone are often the subject of studies and researches. It also happens to meet people with a charisma that fascinates those around them, or people whose communication skills are such as to illuminate or guide other people.

What is it that unites the greatest leaders or the most fascinating seducers? The question may seem simple and obvious, but it is not: "They know who they are!"

The main thing we need to focus on is the harmony we have with those who are close to us, with those who speak to us, with whom we relate. Obviously, to establish harmony, empathy, the fundamental thing is safety in itself together with tools and knowledge.

Another important parameter regarding seduction is related to transmitting emotions. Seduction is not a perfect science in all its constructs, but we must understand that each person is unique in all respects. Let's say that there are common methods or attitudes that allow a simpler means of entering the game of seduction, but without security in us, expectations will be very lacking.

It is good to underline, however, that seduction starts from the principle that success or failure depends on us, on our actions, on the way we act, on the style, and on the moment we act.

Seduction depends on recognizing the resources that we have in us, our original being, in empathizing with the person in front of us, transmitting emotions and not falling into common errors which would highlight our person in a lackluster and uninteresting way and then from what we believe in ourselves from self-esteem. Another detail is also to allow the other person time to seduce as seduction is also a game, and as such, it is necessary to leave space for both persons and allow both to transmit and have emotions.

The psychological mechanisms of seduction have been schematized and linked to archetypes proposed for many centuries in legends and novels but also in works for theater or cinema. There are very different and opposing methods to generate seduction; that is, there are known conditions aimed at creating a more or less balanced exchange of favors of different nature, which leads to a more or less conscious negotiation, declared or tacit.

This variability from person to person and from situation to situation leads many to suppose that seduction does not exist consciously. Therefore, the psychological mechanisms would be the result of the unconscious and not controllable, thus making human courtship fall within those existing in the animal world.

The main mechanism is that one of empathy; the seducer puts himself in the same situation as the seduced person, becomes the victim of the same persecution, shares the same social condition or working activity, participates in the same political struggle, propagates the same religious faith, etc.

Obviously, there are less extreme, or rather almost less, degrees of empathy, such as that which is observable, always in the cinematographic field, in the film Luna di gall where the protagonist gives his bus ticket to a passenger without it and gets fined instead of her.

Another seduction mechanism is that of showing off one's prodigality: resources are wasted on expensive spirits and foods, in roses, and in any type of good and non-lasting service. The mechanism inherent in this behavior (more or less calculated) is that of the exaltation of the "fleeting moment" implicitly, or explicitly, it declares itself to the loved one: this is the most beautiful moment of my life, so far, I have never lived, and not feeling worthy of you, I celebrate the moment before it vanishes.

The perfume has always occupied a pre-eminent role in seduction: it has the magical power to arouse new sensations and emotions that fascinate our senses; it is a subtle weapon, which like all-penetrating weapons, you must know how to dose, choose, use wisely, linking your image to a decisive perfume, which should not change, at lightning rates, as happens instead, in our time, where everything, images, ideas, fashion, is burnt within a season or two, from marketing, from the lack of rules of behavior, intimate and outward, from a race so fast that it becomes anguish, which leaves very little space for games and to express the art of seduction.

Some species of birds sing beautiful songs or dance gracefully around the female they have chosen. Many animals clash in deadly duels to decide who the contested female belongs to. Other species, such as the peacock, unfold their tail to show all their splendor and beauty. Courtship rituals are present throughout the natural world.

Man does not escape this logic; he even repeats in his own way the strategies of other animal species. He shows off his skills, competes for the object of his love with others, and struts, all ways to be able to attract the attention of the possible prey.

According to a biological approach, the presence of the alpha male also dominates the world of humans. It is not really about the individual with the most muscles or the one who risks the skin in a confrontation. The alpha male in today's culture is the one who proves most gifted, who survives, and who imposes himself—the most confident, the one who keeps everything under control, the one who has the first and last words.

This type of man represents the typical "western male." Numerous researches show that it is the one preferred by women, despite feminism.

How to Seduce Him

Many women are unable to show off their best qualities to seduce a man. Often, they are intimidated or are unable to fully understand male psychology, risking to assume absolutely wrong and unprofitable attitudes. In many cases, for example, the woman tends to be polite and helpful in order to fulfill every desire of the courted man. However, in this way, it does nothing but removes the object of desire, who feels "hunted" by a woman of this type, considering her intrusive and inappropriate. In other words, this strategy compromises any possible sexual tension, completely canceling any male desire. The more you trust yourself and the more determined you show yourself, the greater the chances that the man of your dreams will notice and appreciate you.

On the other hand, if you want to trap a certain subject, you will do well to become good listeners: instead of filling it with chatter, trying to persuade him that you are the perfect woman for him, try to pay attention to what your interlocutor says. If you are able to listen to him intelligently, as well as make him being appreciated, you will also be able to understand what he really likes and what his real needs are. An appropriate game of looks that communicates understanding and complicity, moreover, can prove particularly useful to conquer the man of your desires.

Of course, taking care of your physical appearance is also fundamental to seduce a man; in fact, it is known that the first attraction comes from there. Furthermore, once the obstacle of the first contact has been overcome, it is important to know how to open up spontaneously. For example, sharing sexual fantasies could be very intriguing and thus favoring the continuation of dating. In fact, creating expectations regarding the erotic sphere is fundamental to keep a high interest and stimulate mutual attraction.

Don't scare your partner with long-term plans: don't be hasty and, especially in the early days, don't start oppressing him with your plans for the future. In this way, in fact, you will only terrify him and, as soon as you go away to the bathroom to redo your make-up, he will take advantage of it to escape!

Knowing how to speak the standard language correctly, you can also be very beautiful, but if when you open your mouth, you cannot put two words on the cross, your loved one will immediately lose interest in you. In fact, know that men are very daffodils and want to exhibit a trophy that is not only beautiful to look at: when they "present you in society" in fact, they strongly desire to make a good impression. Good command of the language and the ability to speak on any topic are therefore vital to increase your seductive ability.

Act on impulse by eliminating the paranoia; if you instinctively want to talk to a man and approach him, don't think about it too much, but just do it. Spontaneity is definitely the best way to propose yourself to the man who has captured your interest, setting aside, at least in the initial phase, any type of calculation and strategy.

How to Seduce Her

Knowing how to conquer a woman impeccably does not require any type of degree or special recognition. Despite this, most men are unable to seduce the woman of their dreams in the correct way, thus losing the opportunity to seduce her and make a break in her heart.

Often it is associated with knowing how to conquer with physical beauty or muscles, but we can assure that to most women, this is not enough because they are more attracted to the character, and the way of doing that make a woman fall in love. Women are known as the ones liking to be seduced and conquered in an elegant and impeccable way.

If you want to increase your seduction skills and avoid falling into the dreaded friend zone, remember the following tips:

- **Listen to her problems and make her talk about herself:** That women like to talk, and talk is not new, but finding a man who can listen to them and give them useful advice is not easy. Precisely for this reason, when they find one, they hardly let it get away: a woman who tells herself in a transparent and sincere way means that she undoubtedly wants to deepen her knowledge maybe with a second date!

- **Show all your security:** Women love self-confident men who are not afraid to make their own decisions. Whether it is the choice of a restaurant, a destination for a trip, or a decision of one's private life, women love to feel protected and reassured at all times.

- **Be positive:** Positive men have an edge; they manage to enter a woman's heart more simply and sincerely. Positivity is a gift that not all men have, and it is often this that conquers a woman, making her laugh and allowing her to forget all the problems of life.

- **Have a good sense of humor:** Men who are too serious after a while risk getting fed up with women. They like to take everything lightly, especially love relationships; for this reason, seeing their man make his life a little less "heavy" is an excellent advantage.

- **Make her feel important:** The more importance is given to a woman, the more fascinated she will become, behaving accordingly. Making her a part of his decisions, his thoughts, and what he wants from life by asking for advice and opinions is a great way for a man to conquer.

- **Make it a part of your life:** Women know how to be an excellent reference point in a man's life. Even during the first dates, if a man shares his daily life with his woman, she will know how to reward him and make the right contribution. It is an almost foolproof technique for most women, capable of completely dropping them at her feet.

- **Don't overdo the compliments:** Compliments are a great way to "approach" a woman and a nice way to start the conversation, but they certainly should not be exaggerated and too frequent; otherwise, you could risk getting the opposite effect and dismiss the woman of your dreams, losing any opportunity with her.

- **Make her feel desired:** When you try to conquer a woman, you do everything to get her and make her fall in love. Obviously, sensuality and desire play a very important role in the final success. Women like to feel sensual and at the same time desired by a man, making everything even more intriguing and fun.

CHAPTER 4:

Best Sex Positions for Kama Sutra

Different sexual positions are created to enable you to explore the body of your partner and discover the things that make each partner go over the edge.

Something that is perfect for the first time you and your partner have sex.

Finding different ways to make your partner orgasm is arousing on its own.

Introduce new sexual positions in the bedroom to bond further with your partner and communicate the various sexual positions you wish to try because otherwise, your partner will never know what adventure you will wish to embark on in your next sexual session.

Some of the most amazing sex positions that are pleasurable for both men and women are the following ones:

The Milk and Water Embrace

The first Kama Sutra position we will look at is The Milk and Water Embrace. This position gets its name from the idea that the two people in this position are enmeshed and become so close that they lose themselves in the other person.

Interestingly, this position can be used as a loving embrace after sex or as a sexual position itself of you add penetration to it.

The man sits on the edge of the bed, his legs planted on the floor. The woman approaches him and climbs into his lap, her face to his. She wraps her legs around his waist and her arms around his neck. He holds onto her by wrapping his arms around her back.

From here, she positions herself so that she is open enough to receive his penis, and she can help guide him inside of her.

To thrust, they can work together by having the man use his feet on the floor as support.

While the man moves his hips up and down, and the woman grinds her hips on his lap, which allows for clitoral stimulation with the base of the man's penis.

If she wants, the woman can touch her clitoris to stimulate it herself, or if she wants to remain pressed against the man, she can keep both arms around his neck for a closer embrace while her clitoris is stimulated by penetration.

Either way, a blended orgasm is highly possible, as she has the potential to experience both a clitoral and vaginal orgasm at the same time.

The Lotus

This position allows for multiple female orgasms because it involves penetration as well as clitoral stimulation. The man will sit cross-legged, and the woman will sit on his lap, wrapping her legs around behind him. This can be done in a comfortable chair or on a bed. Once the penis is inside of the woman's vagina, he can thrust into her with his hips or lift her up and down on his penis with his arms. Then, since her legs are spread wide in a cross-legged position, she can use a vibrator on her clitoris (or her hand if she doesn't have one). This position will make for possible G-Spot stimulation along with the clitoral stimulation, which can lead to a blended orgasm. It can also lead to back-to-back orgasms. This can happen if she comes clitorally, and then penetration continues, which could then lead to a G-Spot orgasm (or general vaginal orgasm). Then, there is even the possibility of her having another clitoral orgasm if she begins stimulating her clitoris again.

The Tigress

This is another position that allows for the possibility of multiple female orgasms. To set into this position, the man lies down on the bed on his back, and the woman straddles his penis, facing his feet instead of his head. From this position, the woman can grind her hips on the man's penis and control the speed and depth of penetration. To make it a position that allows for a blended orgasm, however, she will lean forward and can grab onto his ankles for support. Then, he can begin to stimulate her anus using his fingers or a sex toy. He does not need to penetrate her anally; he can just play with the outside of her anus, and she will still feel immense amounts of pleasure. If she does wish for penetration to occur both anally and vaginally, she may be able to have a blended orgasm in this way also.

Doggie Style

This is the position men prefer for naughty and dirty sex. The woman should be placed on her hands and knees as the man penetrates her from behind.

Scissor Position

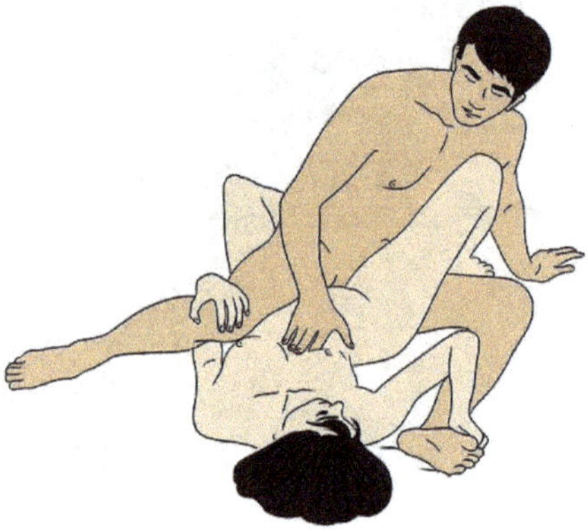

The woman lays on her side, and the man is lying on his side. Both of them are facing each other while in this position. The woman should put her leg over the top leg of the man so as for him to be between her legs with both of his legs together. The woman can arch her back outward or grab the man from around his waist.

G Spot Position

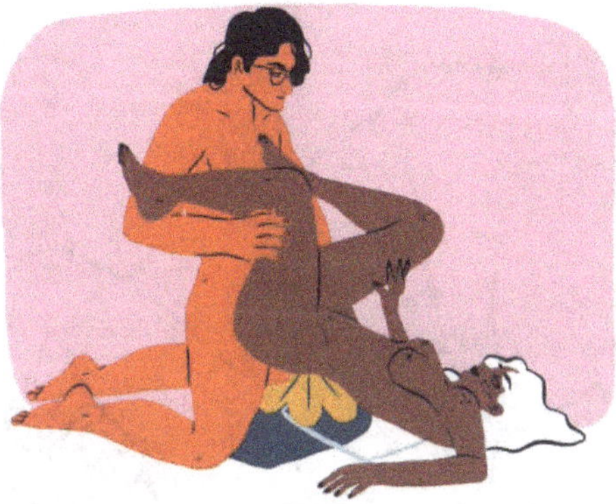

The woman faces down, and the man is straddling her legs so that he can be positioned between her legs.

Missionary Position

This is the basic position that women love. This position will most probably be the one you will use for the first time you have sex with your partner and the easiest one. The girl has to lie on her back with the man on top of her. The man has complete control over the intercourse since the woman is on her back. To make this position more enjoyable, you can put the woman's one or two legs on your shoulders since that will make you go deeper inside her and hit areas that you wouldn't be able to if you are doing a regular missionary position. Her legs could be on the side with her back flat on the bed and her bottom twisted over. With this position, the man will be able to hit her G spot easier.

Forward Spooning Position

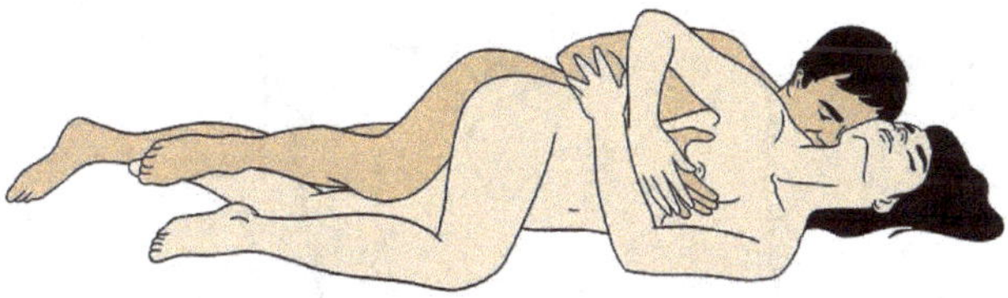

This is a variation of the spooning position and very easy too. The woman and man face each other as they lay on their sides. This position is more intimate. In this position, the man will do most of the work and has to position himself a bit lower than the girl to get inside her easily. If he is taller than average, the man can try to be a bit higher than most, but it would still be a good idea for the man to be located a bit lower than the woman. This position is recommended for a slower pace since it can be hard in this position to get deep inside the woman but still find spots that will please her immensely. The man can kiss her neck and play with her breasts to make the woman climax faster.

Pushup Position

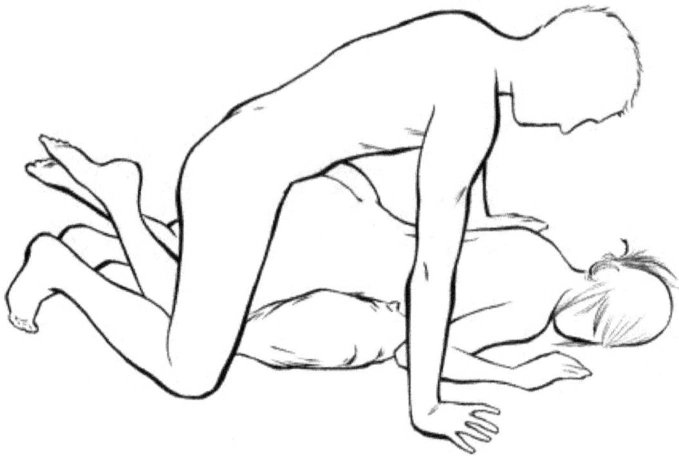

As the name suggests, the man is in a pushup position as he is having intercourse with the woman. Even though the man will remain in this position as he is making love to the woman, the woman can change positions. She can either be on her back with her legs in the air, which will allow for deep penetration. This is an amazing position that you and your partner will seek to do more often. Another variation of this position is when the woman is on her stomach with her butt up in the air. This way, the man can go as fast as he wants and as deep as he wants without stopping. The butt will work as a cushion to help him bounce.

69 Position

This is one of the most popular sex positions. This is a great position for both gay and straight relationships. It aims for oral pleasure, and it is fairly easy to explain and achieve. One partner is on his or her back while the other person lies on top of them in a reversed position. In this position, both partners can be pleasured at the same time while having sex. The woman can get eaten while the man can have his penis sucked. The woman can use her mouth, and the man can use his tongue.

Face Sitting Position

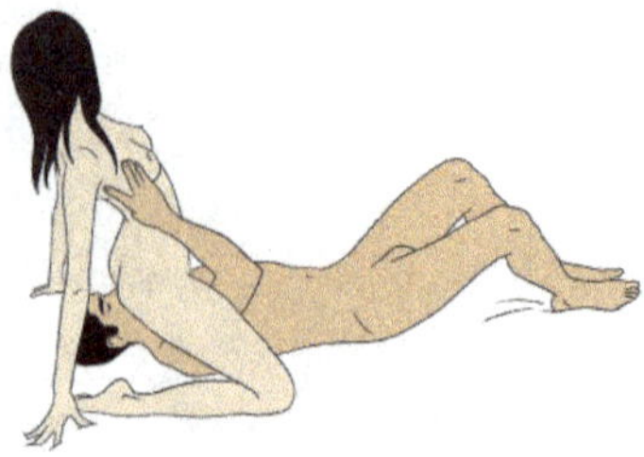

In this position, the man will lay on his back, and the woman places her vagina sitting on his face. This position is meant to offer pleasure to the woman. This is a very easy position, and it must be done before intercourse. The woman can be facing either forward or backward during this position. The man should use his mouth and tongue to stroke her vagina so that she will feel pleasure. Licking and sucking will bring even greater pleasure to the woman, and she will be wet in no time. If the man wishes to get more adventurous, he can play with her butt hole. If so, before the man does that, he should ask the woman first because she may not like such things. While the man is eating the woman out, he could also grab her butt since it will intensify the pleasure she is feeling. He could also spank her to help her get off faster.

The Rocking Horse

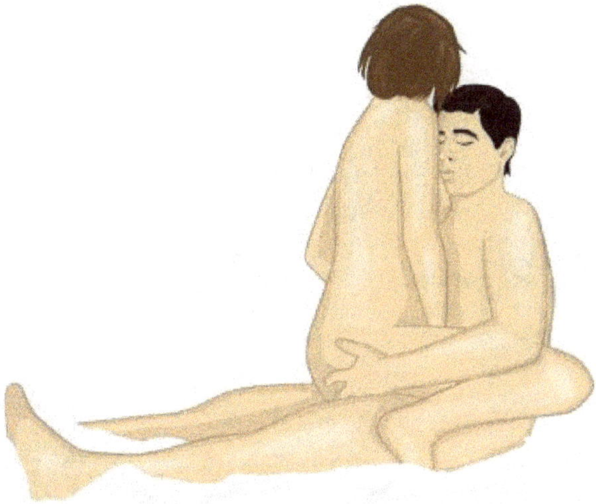

This is a variation of the missionary position with the woman on top that allows her to have total control over the movements. This is also an intimate position that allows the partners to look into each other's eyes and cuddle as they are making love. The man can also take control of the movements. The man can put his arms behind him and lean back as he sits up. His legs can either be straight in front of him or have his knees up and crossed. If the man controls the movements, he can have his knees bent or sit in a position that feels comfortable. The woman will sit on top of the man with a leg on either side of his hips. The woman should be on her knees and rest on her shins for leverage that will help with the movements.

Face Down Position

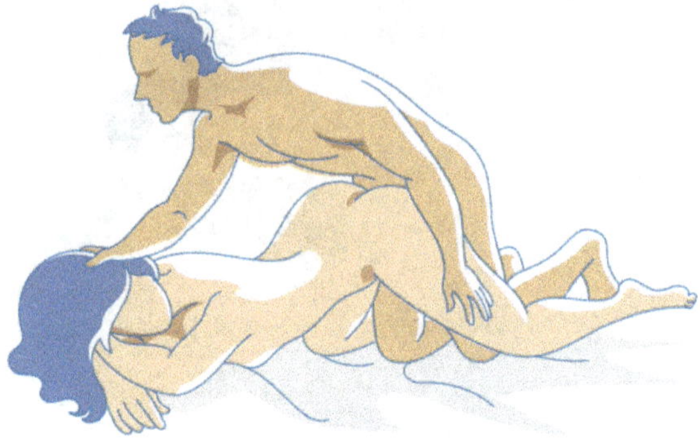

This is another amazing oral sex position that aims to help the woman prepare for a long sexual session. As such, it is meant to give the woman pleasure. The woman should lay on her back either flat or propped up on her elbows. As she is in this position, the man should get on his knees or stomach and place his face right where her vagina is. In this position, the man can suck or lick her vagina. In doing so, the woman will get wet in no time. The man should take care to be gentle with her since this will turn her on more rather than being rough down there. The man can use this time to practice the moves of his tongue and stay there for a long period of time. While the man is eating the woman, he can play with her breasts and kiss the area around her vagina. Women are sensitive and love to be touched in certain areas.

The Rock N Roller Position

This position will offer you the pleasure of face to face and face to back positions. It is a very easy position and can apply to every couple. With this position, the G spot can also be stimulated as he starts gaining deeper penetrations. The woman must lay on her back with her legs in the air. Once the man takes up his position, he must rest her legs on his shoulders. The woman can use a pillow under her head and under her tailbone for extra support and maintain the position comfortable for her. The pillow under the woman's tailbone can make it easier for the man to gain deeper penetration. The man has to scoot in and enter the woman as she places her legs over her shoulders. With this position, the man is in total control, so he can get as deep as he wants and control the movements. The man should always start slowly and move at the woman's pace since entering her too deeply from the beginning can cause her pain and ruin the moment.

The Sidekick

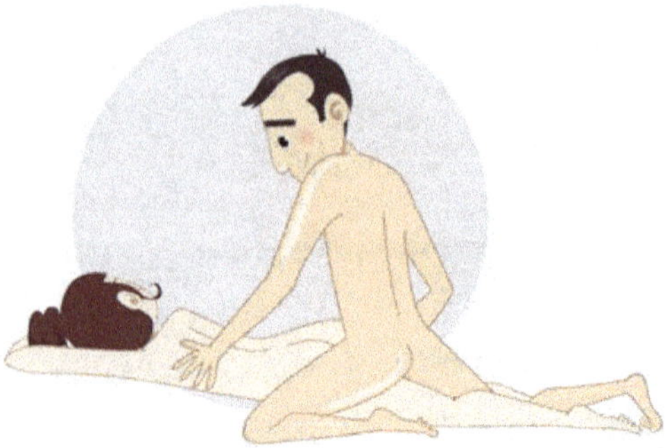

This position also allows the man to enter the woman from behind and has full control of the movements. This pose is very sensual and very relaxing for the woman. With this position, there is a great clitoris stimulation allowed, and it can be easy for the man to leverage his thrusting. The woman should lay on her stomach with her legs straight. She can also bend one knee to the side since this position will add to the stimulation of the clitoris. This position should be relaxing for the woman, so there are not many things that she needs to do other than completely relax. The man should be behind the woman and on his knees to enter her from behind. He can hold her hips to balance himself while thrusting, something that will give him control over how deep he can penetrate her and how fast his movements are. He can also move his hips around to achieve the stimulation of the G spot as well and maximize the pleasure of the woman.

The Closed Door

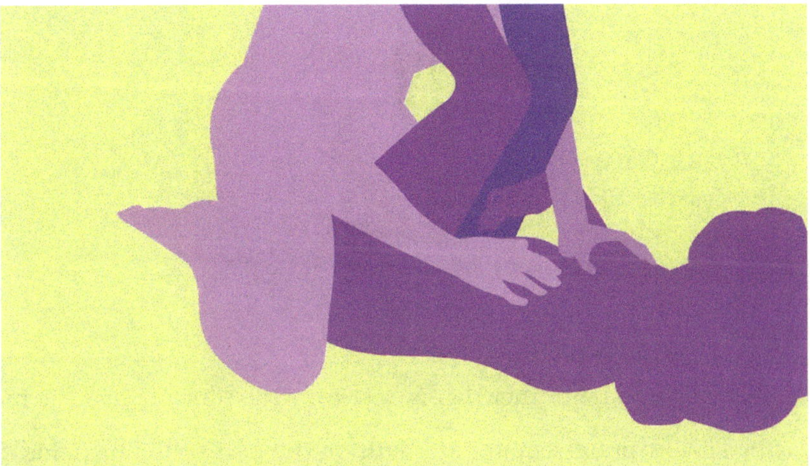

This position is similar to the missionary in that both people are lying down face-to-face, and the man is on top. The difference, however, and what makes this an advanced position is that the woman will keep her legs shut the entire time tightly. The man's penis can be inserted while her legs are open, and then once it is in, she will close her legs. What this does is constrict her vagina and make the canal tighter for the man's penis. In addition to this, if she is aroused, her vagina will be engorged, and the canal will be tighter already. Because of this, the man's penis will be closely hugged as it slides in and out of her, and this will make for extra pleasure for him.

The Lap Dance

This next position is another that is best for male pleasure and the male orgasm. This position requires strength on the part of the man and the woman and is quite an athletic position, but this is why it is called an advanced sex position. Be careful when trying this one.

To get into position, the man will sit upright in a comfortable chair or on the edge of a bed with his feet planted on the floor. The woman will climb onto his lap and wrap her legs around behind the man or stick them straight out past him. Then, the man can insert his penis into the woman's vagina. From here, the woman will lean back until she is lying straight back, and her body is flat. While she does this, the man will have to hold onto her at her hips or her lower back, depending on your height variations. The man in this position will perform a combination of thrusting his hips into the woman from a seated position and pulling her onto his penis repeatedly. A high amount of upper body strength is required on the part of the man in this position. Place some pillows on the floor underneath the woman when trying this position, just in case. The woman can hold onto the man's arms for support as well here.

Splitting the Bamboo

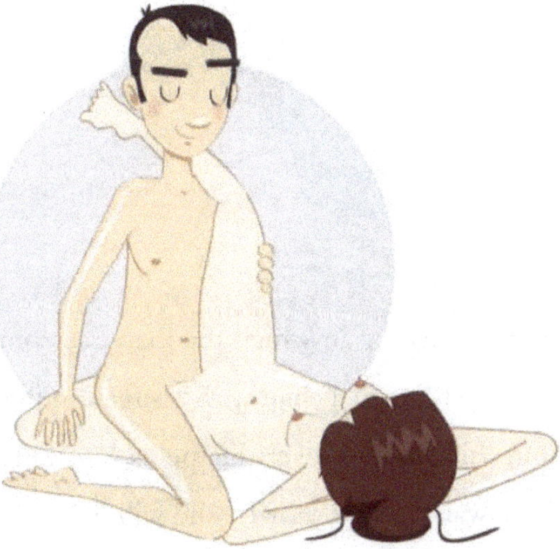

This position is quintessentially Kama Sutra, and it is a great position for the male orgasm.

To get into this position, the woman will lie on her back on the bed and stretch one of her legs straight out below her, lifting the other leg up and resting it on the man's shoulder.

The man will be on top of the woman, his hips between her legs.

The Waterfall

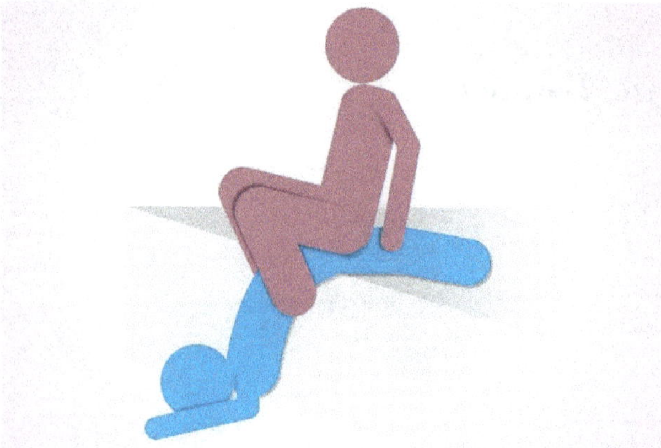

The waterfall is a position in which the man has complete control. The man will begin by sitting in a chair with his feet on the floor. The woman will climb onto his lap and insert his penis into her. She can wrap her legs around his waist. Then, slowly, she will lean all the way back until her head and arms are touching the floor (with pillows underneath). From here, the man will hold onto her hips and can move her body onto his penis at whatever speed and depth he wishes. He can also grab onto her breasts and massage her clitoris in this position if he wishes. This position can be quite challenging for the woman, but the blood flow to her head will make it pleasurable for her. This position is great for the man since he is in control, and the tightness of the woman's vagina around his penis in this position will be greatly pleasurable for him.

Standing Suspended from Behind-Anal

This position is great for those who are experienced with anal sex as it allows for deep penetration and also requires strength from both partners. This one is a bit trickier to get into, so to begin, the man will be sitting down on the edge of the bed or in a chair, and the woman will sit on his lap, facing away from him. Then, the man will insert his penis into her anus. He will hold onto her under her knees or under her buttocks, and once secure, he will stand up, still inside of her. Then, leaning his back against a wall for support, he will thrust into and out of her while holding her up. This position can be very pleasurable for both people if fitness and strength are there, which is why this is such an advanced position. This position is great for the male orgasm because this position and the fact that it involves anal sex will make it feel great for him. The only thing is that it requires a lot of work from the woman as well.

CHAPTER 5:

How to Reach Ecstasy in Different Positions

A genuine puzzle, among other things, because the way we have sex can change the experience. A considerable number of individuals miss innovative climaxes just because they don't analyze them. Try not to look like them. Use this simple manual to discover a place that delights you and your partner.

Stir Up Positions that Allow and Deny Eye Contact

The principal thing to note about sexual positions is that it is much more than merely discovering approaches to enter your sweetheart all the more profoundly. How you position yourself when you have intercourse brings numerous different things into play. Yet, above all, you can either meet as you fuck or lose an eye-to-eye connection. Change back and forth between both, being in control lady and man finding their best sex position.

Test in Various Rooms and Places

The moment you start having sex, do not hand it over to a partner to deal with the force. Positions like that of the preacher require the person to work with more enthusiasm and cut off the degree of communication with the lady. Mixing it with some time in the Cowboy position can allow each partner to shine.

Trial with Standing Positions

Here's another unusual stunt that individuals overlook: Sex doesn't need to occur on the sheets of your bed either. Standing positions like the "Ballet performer" can permit a speedier and more profound entrance.

You should simply stand, confronting one another. Presently, the female partner raises one of her legs as the male enters her straight away. It's speedy, essential, and extraordinary for quick ones.

Concoct a Sexual Feast in the Kitchen

Another good thought is to explore different avenues regarding various rooms of the house. For example, the kitchen is an incredible spot to expand your sexual skylines. The tallness of work surfaces and tables appears to have been planned considering sex.

At the point when you're in the state of mind, put down your spatula, push away your plates and locate a little space to rest. The person should simply turn off the gas and get the chance to work.

Do Some Stretches and Get Athletic

If you have ever seen pornography, you are supposed to know some of the most genuine sexual positions; however, have you ever tried them?

If not, here is the thing to remember that positions like the wheelbarrow are an extraordinary enjoyment. However, they require quality and adaptability.

By all methods, attempt them, yet do a couple of stretches before you do as such, as no one needs to pull a muscle at the essential minute.

There's More than One Way to Come from Behind

For some individuals, sex from behind is doggy-style, yet that is crazy. Doggy, for the most part, includes accepting a creeping position. However, you can likewise try different things with the Flatiron. Right now, lie face down with straight legs, at that point marginally raise their hips, making an erotically bent profile that folks can't help it. It's an incredible small variation from a stale old position.

Make sure to Watch Your Speed and Power

At the point when you begin evaluating diverse sexual positions, recall that your partner will encounter new sensations. You may be entering her more profound than at any other time.

You may be reaching a climax more quickly, or you may be in a comfortable situation. It could be uncomfortable in the remote possibility of you pushing too hard and too fast, so be aware of what it says and locate the ideal harmony for each position.

Utilize Your Shoulders for Faster, More Efficient Orgasms

Sex is actually about climaxes when you get down to it; however, here's the entertaining thing: most folks have no idea which positions carry ladies to climax the quickest. One approach to do so is by working your shoulders into your daily sexual practice.

Attempt positions like The Fusion, which includes your accomplice, putting her legs on your shoulders. If she gets drained, you can change to The Spider, with her feet on the bed once more. It's an incredible method to make variety in the vibe of the encounter, which assists with making quicker, progressively energetic peaks.

Get Far Out with the Snow Angel

Some of the time, trying different things with sex positions can appear to be peculiar, yet don't accept that because a situation seems to be weird, it won't work. Take the Snow Angel, for instance.

Here, you lie looking in inverse ways, and the man infiltrates "backward" as the lady sees his rear end rising and falling. The opposite penetration is an astonishing inclination, and there's consistently scope for a rim job if all works out positively.

Oral Sex for Him and For Her

Now everyone has their views and opinions when it comes to oral sex. What one needs to understand is that when you are looking to experiment with sex and do things differently, you should surely try and opt for oral sex.

Oral sex is a great way to create the right movement and to keep things mighty exciting, and pump up the passion in the relationship as well. When you are really into it, you are not likely to think of things like how icky this is or is it even hygienic.

Be Vocal

Don't just do it; let your partner feel every bit of it. A good sexy narration of what you are doing to the insides of their body with your magical tongue is a great way to keep the sex hormones surging higher and higher until the body may reach the climax. So, when you are licking the insides of her vagina or even when you are giving your man the perfect blowjob, be all set to give a sexy narration of how it feels when your moth touches their insides, and don't forget to add in a little moan here and there for all that extra glitz.

The Background Porn

Now, this depends on both the partners and how much they are willing to use this. However, a lot of couples have hinted that watching porn together acts like a great stimulant and helps them fall in the feel a lot more easily.

So, when you are administering oral sex to your partner, you could have an oral sex porn clip playing on your television. The music, the ambiance, and the video sometimes set the right tempo and get you both in the real mood.

The Play of Hot Breath

Now, this seems to be a scientific fact. When you use your hot breath on the intimate openings of your partner, it is likely to create a wave of stimulation to the nerve endings. So, try to puff out a breath of hot air on the vagina and then let the tongue take her for a ride. Trust me; she is going to dig her nails all over you and moan and call out your name in a way you will never ever forget.

Mix and Match

When we talk of oral sex, it doesn't really have to be limited to just the play of your mouth. For some of the best excitement and results, you could mix and match it up, let your fingers go deep inside her, and then pull them out sharply. Do not let her breathe. Go further and kiss the insides of her vagina and lick her as if your whole world depends on it.

This in and out movement and the mix and match of fingers and tongue is sure to drive any woman crazy, and she is going to ask for more and more. Remember, the idea is to keep teasing her until she wants nothing more but the whole of you inside her.

Use Lube if Needed

Some of us tend to have it too dry, both men and women included. Feel free to make exciting use of lube. There are several sweet-smelling massage oils available too. Look for massage porn, if the need be. Try to lubricate the parts totally, and then give a gentle massage. This often builds the whole tempo, and then you can slowly tease your partner and let your mouth do the rest of the magic.

So, these are some of the best tips which you can use to get the most out of oral sex. If you haven't yet done it, this is the time to try it now. Tonight, show some of the sexiest oral sex moves to your partner and watch them moan on and on in pleasure.

How to Overcome Insecurities in the Bedroom

There are many reasons why a person may feel insecure in the bedroom. This can be because of their body image, their performance, or their ability to please their partner. Below are some ways to deal with these insecurities.

Communication is the key to a fulfilling and pleasurable sex life. Knowing what you and your partner like and dislike allow you to focus on the things you enjoy and leave the things you don't behind. Knowing this will help to greatly reduce your anxiety surrounding performance or being able to please your partner adequately. With so many options for ways to pleasure each other, you don't want to waste time on the things that don't make you scream out of pleasure, and communication is the way! During sex is an important time to check in with your partner to see how they are feeling, what they are liking, and what they want more of. While you are having sex, it is easiest to communicate using dirty talk so that you don't ruin the mood by coming off too serious or too concerned. In order to properly communicate while also playing into the mood of the moment, you can do so in a sexy way, using sexy language. You should tell each other what you like by saying, "oh yes, I like that" or "I like when you touch me like that" This lets the person know to do more of the same because this is what will get you to orgasm. By being aware of these things and being able to talk about them at the moment, it will help with your confidence in the bedroom and reduce your insecurities.

How to Overcome Anxiety in the Bedroom

It is very common for people to have anxiety in the bedroom, especially around things like orgasm and performance. There are some ways that you can reduce your orgasm and performance anxiety in the bedroom.

Your choice of environment can make a big difference when it comes to whether or not you can reach orgasm. If you tend to be someone who has trouble reaching orgasm for whatever reason, these details of the environment, the location, and the time will be important for your experience. They will determine whether or not you will be able to get concentrated enough to orgasm. We will discuss several factors that contribute to whether or not your environment is conducive to your pleasure and your orgasm. The reason why the environment, time and location are of such importance is that being comfortable with all of these factors will allow you to focus on yourself, your pleasure and your orgasm without distraction.

CHAPTER 6:

Tips to Improve Your Sex Life

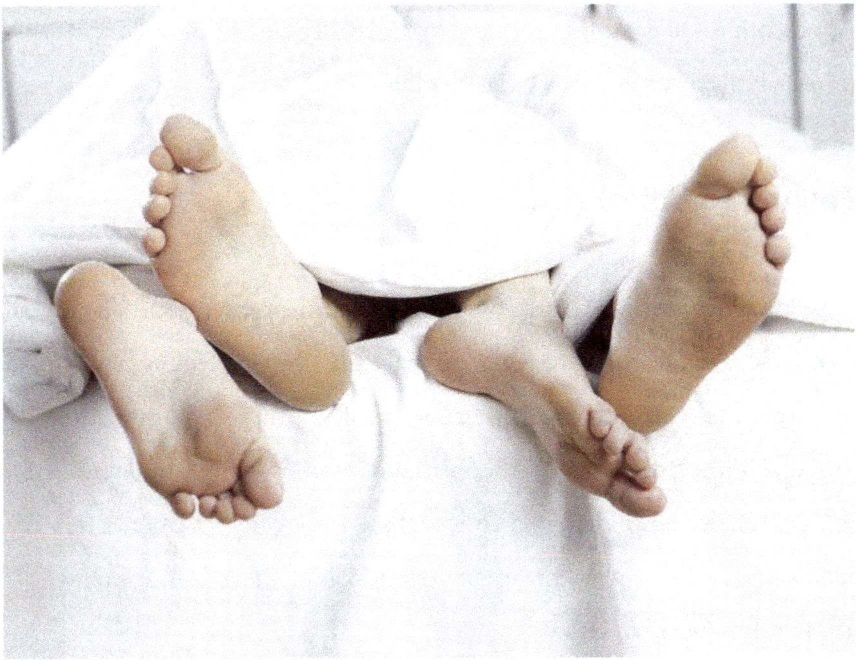

Enjoying More Fulfilling Sex

Whether the issue is big or small, there are a lot you can do to get your sex life going. The overall mental, physical and emotional wellbeing goes hand in hand with your sexual well-being. Contact your partner, keep your lifestyle safe, use some of the many excellent self-help materials on the market and enjoy the weather will help you.

Achieve a Satisfying Sex Life

Sex. The word can evoke an emotional kaleidoscope. Through passion, anticipation, tenderness to loneliness, apprehension, and deceit, the reactions themselves are just as varied as sexual experiences. Therefore, in the course of a sex life lasting many decades several people will come across all these feelings and many others.

Talking to Your Spouse

Most people find it difficult even under the best circumstances to talk about sex. When there are sexual problems, feelings of pain, embarrassment, remorse and anger will completely interrupt the conversation. Because good communication is the foundation of a healthy relationship, dialog is an initial step not only to a better sex life, but as well to a more emotional relationship. Here are some tips to resolve this sensitive issue.

Find the Right Time to Talk

There are two different kinds of sexual conversations: those in the bedroom and those elsewhere. It's perfectly easy to tell your partner what's nice about lovemaking, but it's better to wait until you're more rational to think about bigger issues such as sex or orgasmic disruptions.

Avoid Criticism

Positive couched ideas, like, "I love it when you brush my hair gently," instead of dwelling on negative things. Approach a sexual problem as a problem to be solved rather than a fault assigning exercise together.

Trust Your Partner About Your Body Changes

If you're holding hot flashes at night or menopause leaves your vagina dry, talk about these things with your friend. It's much better to know what really is happening instead of viewing such physical changes as being uninteresting. Even, if you are a guy and you don't just get an erection from the sex thinking, teach your wife how to stimulate you instead of making her think that she is not as beautiful as to excite you.

Be Trustworthy

Be honest. You may think that you are defending the feelings of your partner by faking an orgasm, but in fact you start a slippery slope. As daunting as any sexual issue is, the problem skyrockets when the problem is lying, hurt, and frustration.

Don't Associate Love With Sexual Performance

Build a loving and tenderness environment, always touch and kiss. Don't blame your own sexual problems or your partner. Concentrate instead on preserving the relationship emotional and physical intimacy. Another potentially sensitive issue worth discussing for older couples is what will happen after a partner die. The surviving partner is likely to want to find a new partner in couples who have a healthy sex life. Expressing your openness towards this choice while you both live would possibly alleviate culpability and make the surviving partner's experience less difficult.

Use Self-help Techniques

It is easier than ever to use self-help approaches to address sexual problems. If you need them, there are innovative medications and professional sex therapists. But you can fix minor sexual problems by making some changes to your lovemaking style. Here are some things at home that you can do.

Educate Yourself

Educate yourself. Some good self-help resources for every type of sexual issue are available. Browse the Internet and choose some resources to help you and your partner better understand the problem. If it's too hard to talk directly, you and your partner should highlight passages you really like and show each other.

Give Yourself Time

Give yourself time. Your sexual impulses slow down as you get older. You and your partner will improve your chances of success by finding a quiet, relaxed and uninterrupted sex setting. Remember, realize that the physical changes in your body take longer to be awakened and to reach orgasm. If you think about it, spending more time having sex is not bad; it can open doors to a different kind of sexual experience by engaging with these physical needs in the lovemaking routine.

Practice Touching

The responsive concentration strategies used by sex therapists will allow you to regain physical intimacy without being under pressure. You may also want to ask your partner to contact you to reach him or her. However, this will give you a better idea of how much pressure you should use, from gentle to strong.

CHAPTER 7:

Ways to Make You Last Longer in Bed

So, this is more of a recap with a few new ideas thrown in for good measure. At the end of the day, most men want to be able to last longer in bed, not just those who suffer from premature ejaculation. We all know it isn't any fun for either of you when things end too quickly but, on the other hand, all the media hype that says you should be going at it for half an hour or more is also wrong. Many men are conscious of the fact that they may be finishing just a little too quickly for their partner as all those Hollywood movies and magazines would have you believe women love sessions that go on for hours.

Back to Your Teenage Years

Remember how, as a teenager, you used to spend what felt like hours kissing and making out without actually having sex? Felt good, didn't it. So, go back to doing that. Spend more time on kissing your partner, on exploring each other using your hands and your mouth before you even think about actually having sex.

Learn How to Massage

When you lead a busy life, it becomes quite difficult to find the time for sex and it isn't easy to make the move from your busy working life to a sexy erotic one. Stress is the culprit here and before you can even begin to feel like getting down to it, you need to de-stress. The very best way to do that is through massage, and if you do it properly, both you and your partner will be completely turned on by it. You do need to learn how to do this properly, though; if you don't you can actually cause more problems. Learn to give a very deep and satisfying massage and then each of you takes about 5 or 10 minutes to massage each other before you think about sex. Not only are you really getting in the mood, but you will be helping each other to breathe properly and to relax. Foot and back messages are perfect for priming you for pleasure and comfort and, think of it this way – each minute you spend intimately massaging your partner is another minute towards your goal of lasting longer in bed.

Take It in Turns

Most sexual sessions are pretty much a give and take pleasure method, in which each of you touches each other at the same time, which means you are both heading for the finish line pretty darn quick. There is a golden rule here if you really want things to take longer – take it in turns to touch each other.

From now on, let your partner do the touching while you relax, lie back and take as much pleasure from it as you can without getting too over-excited. Then return the favor; let her lie back while you do the touching and exploring. Both of you need to learn how to use your hands properly to give as much pleasure as possible, leading both of you down the road to arousal but not so quick as it would normally happen.

Control Your Surroundings

The truth of the matter is when you are in a comfortable position, in comfortable surroundings, a place where either you or your partner is likely to get too over excited, you are more likely to last longer in bed. Don't be tempted with public sex or anything else that could be just that little too exciting for you. If your most comfortable place for sex is in bed then keep it in the bedroom, at least until you have learned how to control your orgasm.

Use the Start-Stop Technique

With this technique, your woman will stimulate you until you start to get close to an orgasm. At this point, tell her that she must stop. When your levels of sexual tension have reduced, it could be as quick as 15 seconds, start again. By doing this frequently, not only will you last longer for that particular session, but you will also begin to understand your own feelings and will learn how to stop yourself.

Learn to Breathe From the Belly

When you breathe deeply, it is actually a direct correlation to ejaculation. So, breathing deeply and slowly should help you to reduce stress and anxiety, thus slowing down your rate of ejaculation. Learn how to breathe so that your belly will rise before your chest does and practice this in conjunction with the start-stop technique.

Read the Kama Sutra

Preferably together as this will heighten the pleasure for both of you. Plus, you could always try out some of the positions! In all seriousness, though, there is a specific technique that is mentioned that can help you to stay the distance.

Using this technique, start off very slowly, with just one in and out stroke per three seconds.

Then you can begin to build up the strokes, adding in more, over a session of about four or five minutes until you are at the stage where you are giving one stroke per second. If you feel as if you are about to lose control, stop, stay inside your woman until you regain control and then start from the beginning again

Out of Your Head

And I do not mean on drugs or alcohol! One of the biggest killers during sex, the one thing that will affect whether you can maintain an erection or not, is stress. And that comes down to what is going through your mind. In the case of premature ejaculation or in those who seem to rush it all the time, the main thoughts are going to be on your abilities and your performance and that will likely push you over the edge.

Learn how to change your thinking to positivity and confidence pushing worry and stress out of the way. If you start to feel anxious or stressed during sex, stop, breathe deeply and then focus on your inner self. Get rid of the negative thoughts and put your attention firmly on you and your feelings.

Learn to Control Your Ejaculatory Muscle

When you ejaculate, do you ever wonder what physically causes it to happen? There is a specific muscle that controls your ejaculation and, when it is relaxed, you simply cannot ejaculate, no matter how hard you try. We talked about it earlier – it's called the PC muscle and it what is responsible for letting the semen come out when you come.

To control your rate of ejaculation, you have to know how to control this muscle. Practice the exercises we talked about earlier as much as you can until you have almost full control over it. This won't be instant; it can take as much as four weeks to get really good results. It will also take a great deal of regular practice to get it right and become a sexual master.

Learn How to Cool Down

Whether you suffer from premature ejaculation or not, you should still learn a few methods for cooling down. You can practice these so that, if you do find yourself heading towards being out of control you can stop yourself before you do go over the edge. Do your research and find the methods that will work for you that will help you to last a bit longer in bed.

Change It Up

What is the absolute best thing you can do when you find yourself heading fast toward that point of no return? The biggest piece of advice that I can give you is to change your speed. Men should have a go at teasing their partners; remove your tool from inside her and rub the head up and down over her sex.

are a lot of nerve endings there and this will make her feel great, as well as help to slow you down a bit.

Squeeze

There are three areas that, when squeezed, can help to slow you down and keep you hard. First, when your penis is erect, make a ring with your index finger and your thumb around the base of it and squeeze it. This stimulates a ring around the base of the penis which helps to keep the blood where it should be. The second place is underneath the head of the penis. Applying pressure there can work wonders as it is the hot spot in most men and is full of nerve endings. Lastly, the perineum, the spot that is located in between the anus and the base of your testicles.

All of these techniques are designed for you, with you in mind. Obviously, you don't need to do all of what you have learned in this book, just what you feel comfortable doing, what makes you and your partner feel good and what works. Basically, do whatever it takes to make your bedtime sessions last as long as you both want them to.

Conclusion

The Kama Sutra is the epitome of an intimate sexual relationship. This has covered all of the basics, especially about how the Kama Sutra is more than just sex. It is about the connection with your partner on an emotional and spiritual level. This book is written to teach a novice about how to set the mood and how to hold your partner, with a few positions to try out.

The Kama Sutra is about loving your partner and showing them by exploring every inch of their body. It is not about being considered a "sex god" but about being an attentive lover.

It's an exact series of steps that allow and provide to others the wellness and understanding that you should have with yourself and with others. As you see, Tantric sex is one of the best ways to bolster the relationship that you have with the person that you love, and if you feel like you could benefit from tantric sex, then try it.

Creating your unique language of love is not as hard as it seems. Look at your lover and think about all the things that you find attractive about them—all the things you love. Focus on the aspects of them that trigger your lust. The next time you're in bed together, be present and relish the moment. Immerse yourself in the sensation of their tight pussy around your hard penis and vocalize how good it feels. Immerse yourself in the sensation of having his hard, throbbing penis deep inside you and cry out how good it feels. Immerse yourself in the heat of the moment, and the words will eventually come to you. Above all else, be genuine, be honest, and be sincere

What wonder sex can be for a loving couple. When both partners are actively engaged in keeping the flame alive, sex can be the glue that binds them together. When we let that flame die, for whatever reason, our lives together lose something. We become roommates who used to find each other attractive once upon a time and perhaps forget how that happened.

With your unique, combined creativity as a couple, every day is going to be an adventure. Your willingness to explore and to rediscover the people you fell in love with will have you falling in love all over again. There was a time when you couldn't keep your hands off each other, and that time can be now if you're willing to do what it takes to make it happen.

As you go on in your sexual life, stay open-minded, and never stop listening to your body. People change, and you will likely change as well. By being open to these changes and being receptive to them in yourself and your long-term partner, you will be able to ensure you are always getting the most out of sex. Don't forget to communicate with your partners in order to better understand them and sex in general, as communication leads to learning and this is a great thing when it comes to sex.

In as much as you have to be careful and not hurt anybody's feelings, you should also be free—play along with the words. Twist them whichever way you want. If you're just starting out, you can use some of the phrases in the book until you can create your own. Be adventurous and use your words to make your partner horny and aroused.

Let them enjoy it. And if you like to hear others use dirty words, introduce it to your partner gradually. There's no simple rule for sex. All you need to do is to not exceed the personal boundaries of your partner, and you're good to go.

Have a wonderful sex life! `

CPSIA information can be obtained
at www.ICGtesting.com
Printed in the USA
LVHW062010080621
689455LV00038B/1261

9 781803 001593